EIGHTH NOTE PUBLICATIONS

Two Holland Tales

Traditional
Arranged by Ryan Meeboer

Inspired by two folk songs from my Dutch heritage, *Two Holland Tales* is a piece that combines lyrical and upbeat sections. *There Were Two Royal Children* is the opening lyrical movement which displays the talents of most of the parts. Balance is key for this part of the piece, as the melody is moved around the different sections and it is important that it is always heard over the colourful backgrounds.

The piece then moves into *I Once Stood On the Netherland's Hills*. This movement is meant to be fun and played with a light bounce. In the second half of this section, a third Dutch folksong, *Three Nasty Drummers*, is used as a counter-melody by the fourth part and is meant to add some new, interesting material to the piece as it comes to its closing.

ISBN: 9781771578677
CATALOG NUMBER: BQ222544

COST: $15.00
DURATION: 2:50

DIFFICULTY RATING: Easy-Medium
Brass Quintet

TWO HOLLAND TALES

Traditional
Arranged by Ryan Meeboer
There Were Two Royal Children

When I Stood on the Netherlands' Hills

Bb Trumpet 1

TWO HOLLAND TALES

Traditional
Arranged by Ryan Meeboer

There Were Two Royal Children

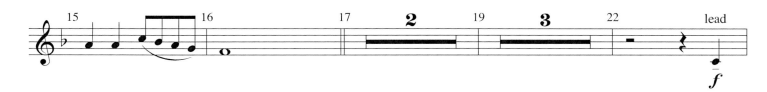

When I Stood on the Netherlands' Hills

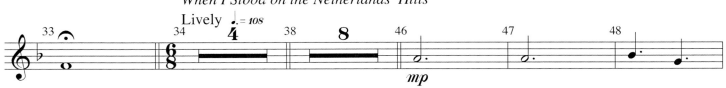

TWO HOLLAND TALES pg. 2

Bb Trumpet 2

TWO HOLLAND TALES

Traditional
Arranged by Ryan Meeboer

TWO HOLLAND TALES pg. 2

F Horn

TWO HOLLAND TALES

Traditional
Arranged by Ryan Meeboer

There Were Two Royal Children

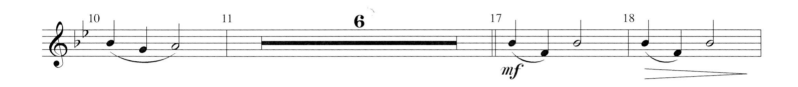

When I Stood on the Netherlands' Hills

TWO HOLLAND TALES pg. 2

Trombone

TWO HOLLAND TALES

Traditional
Arranged by Ryan Meeboer

TWO HOLLAND TALES pg. 2

Tuba

TWO HOLLAND TALES

Traditional
Arranged by Ryan Meeboer

There Were Two Royal Children
More Motion ♩ = 84

When I Stood on the Netherlands' Hills
Lively ♩. = 108